Sara Swan Miller

Turtles

Life in a Shell

Franklin Watts - A Division of Grolier Publishing
New York • London • Hong Kong • Sydney • Danbury, Connecticut

For Ilka List, fellow turtle lover

Photographs ©: Animals Animals: 37 (Zig Leszczynski), 35 (Patti Murray), 43 (Doug Wechsler); Dr. Gerald Kutchling: 27 (The University of Western Australia); Photo Researchers: 5 bottom right (Richard L. Carlton), 15 (Suzanne L. & Joseph T. Collins), 5 top right (Helen Cruickshank), 5 top left (E.R. Degginger), 42 (John Dommers), 5 bottom left (Phil Dotson), cover (Jeff Lepore), 13 (Tom McHugh), 7 top (Paul Metzger), 29 (Larry Miller), 19 (John Mitchell), 40, 41 (Michael Murphy), 33 (David & Hayes Norris), 39 (Jany Sauvanet); Visuals Unlimited: 6 (Bill Beatty), 23 (Patrice Copyright), 7 bottom (Gerald & Buff Corsi), 1 (Arthur Gurmankin), 25 (A. Kerstitch), 16, 17, 20, 21 (Joe McDonald), 31 (Gustav W. Verderber).

Illustrations by Jose Gonzales and Steve Savage

Visit Franklin Watts on the Internet at:
http://publishing.grolier.com

Library of Congress Cataloging-in-Publication Data

Miller, Sara Swan.
Turtles: life in a shell / Sara Swan Miller.
 p. cm. — (Animals in order)
 Includes bibliographical references and index.
 Summary: An introduction to turtles that includes descriptions of fifteen species and recommendations for finding, identifying, and observing them.
  ISBN 0-531-11521-6 (lib.bdg.)   0-531-15947-7 (pbk,)
  1. Turtles—Juvenile literature [1. Turtles.] I. Title. II. Series.
QL666.C5M54   1999
597.92—dc21   98-15260
                                                        CIP
                                                        AC

GROLIER
PUBLISHING

Contents

Is That a Turtle?

If you ask what a turtle is, most people will probably tell you that it is an animal that carries its house around on its back. But just having a shell doesn't make an animal a turtle. Horseshoe crabs, lobsters, clams, and armadillos have shells, too, but they aren't turtles. So just what *is* a turtle?

On the next page are four animals with shells—three turtles and an armadillo. Do you know how the turtles are different from the armadillo? Notice that each of the turtles look very different from one another. Do you know why?

Painted turtle

Gopher tortoise

Nine-banded armadillo

Loggerhead turtle

Traits of Turtles

Although turtles and armadillos look similar, they are not closely related. In fact, an armadillo is more closely related to you than it is to a turtle. Turtles are closely related to snakes, lizards, and crocodiles. All these animals are *reptiles*. They lay eggs on land and they are *cold-blooded*—their body temperature changes as the air temperature of their environment changes. When the air temperature is cold, a turtle's breathing and heartbeat slow down. You are *warm-blooded*. As long as you stay healthy, your body temperature will be about 98.6 degrees Fahrenheit (37° Celsius).

A turtle's shell is made up of two parts. The top part is called the *carapace*, and the bottom part is called the *plastron*. Both are made of bone covered with horny scales, called *scutes*. The carapace and plastron are joined together, with openings for the turtle's legs, head, and tail. If you could look inside its arched carapace, you would see that a

A snapping turtle laying eggs

turtle's backbone and rib cage are part of the shell. Now you know why a turtle never comes out of its shell!

There are two different groups of turtles. A hidden-neck turtle can pull its head directly into its shell. A side-necked turtle must fold its head sideways under its shell.

A turtle's feet are suited to the kind of life it leads. Freshwater turtles have separate toes with claws, and they often have webbing between their toes. The toes of land turtles are fused together—their feet look like an elephant's. Sea turtles have toes that look like flippers.

Turtles first appeared on Earth more than 200 million years ago, and they have changed very little since then. Sadly, these ancient animals are now in trouble. Several species are endangered, mostly because humans are destroying their *habitats*. At the end of this book, you'll find out what people are doing to try to save turtles. Maybe you can help!

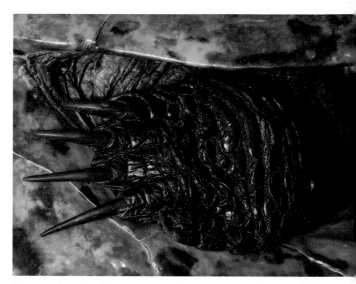

Foot of a freshwater turtle

Foot of a land turtle

The Order of Living Things

A tiger has more in common with a house cat than with a daisy. A true bug is more like a butterfly than a jellyfish. Scientists arrange living things into groups based on how they look and how they act. A tiger and a house cat belong to the same group, but a daisy belongs to a different group.

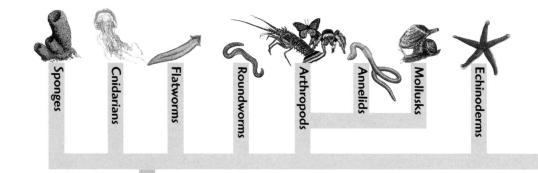

Sponges · Cnidarians · Flatworms · Roundworms · Arthropods · Annelids · Mollusks · Echinoderms

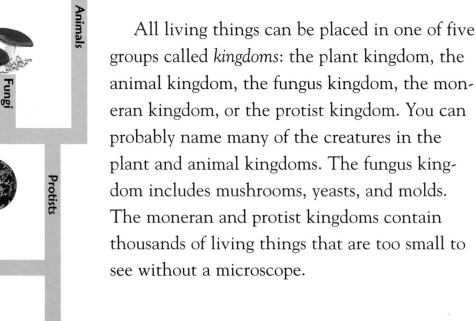

Animals · Plants · Fungi · Protists · Monerans

All living things can be placed in one of five groups called *kingdoms*: the plant kingdom, the animal kingdom, the fungus kingdom, the moneran kingdom, or the protist kingdom. You can probably name many of the creatures in the plant and animal kingdoms. The fungus kingdom includes mushrooms, yeasts, and molds. The moneran and protist kingdoms contain thousands of living things that are too small to see without a microscope.

8

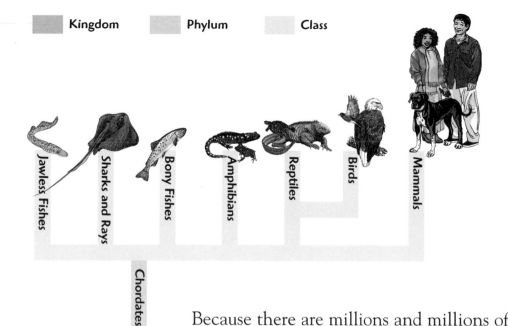

Kingdom　　Phylum　　Class

Jawless Fishes

Sharks and Rays

Bony Fishes

Amphibians

Reptiles

Birds

Mammals

Chordates

Because there are millions and millions of living things on Earth, some of the members of one kingdom may not seem all that similar. The animal kingdom includes creatures as different as tarantulas and trout, jellyfish and jaguars, salamanders and sparrows, elephants and earthworms.

To show that an elephant is more like a jaguar than an earthworm, scientists further separate the creatures in each kingdom into more specific groups. The animal kingdom can be divided into nine *phyla*. Humans belong to the chordate phylum. Almost all chordates have a backbone.

Each phylum can be subdivided into many *classes*. Humans, mice, and elephants all belong to the mammal class. Each class can be further divided into *orders*; orders into *families*, families into *genera*, and genera into *species*. All the members of a species are very similar.

How Turtles Fit In

You can probably guess that turtles belong to the animal kingdom. They have much more in common with swordfish and snakes than with maple trees and morning glories.

Turtles belong to the chordate phylum. Almost all chordates have a backbone and a skeleton. Can you think of other chordates? Examples include elephants, mice, snakes, frogs, birds, fish, and whales.

The chordate phylum can be divided into a number of classes. Turtles belong to the reptile class. As you learned earlier, snakes, lizards, and crocodiles are also reptiles.

There are several different orders of reptiles. Turtles make up one of these orders. The scientific name for this order is testudina, which comes from the Latin word for "arch." As you learned earlier, a turtle has an arched shell, which is connected to its backbone.

Turtles can be divided into a number of different families and genera. These groups can be broken down into hundreds of species. You will learn more about some of the turtles in this book.

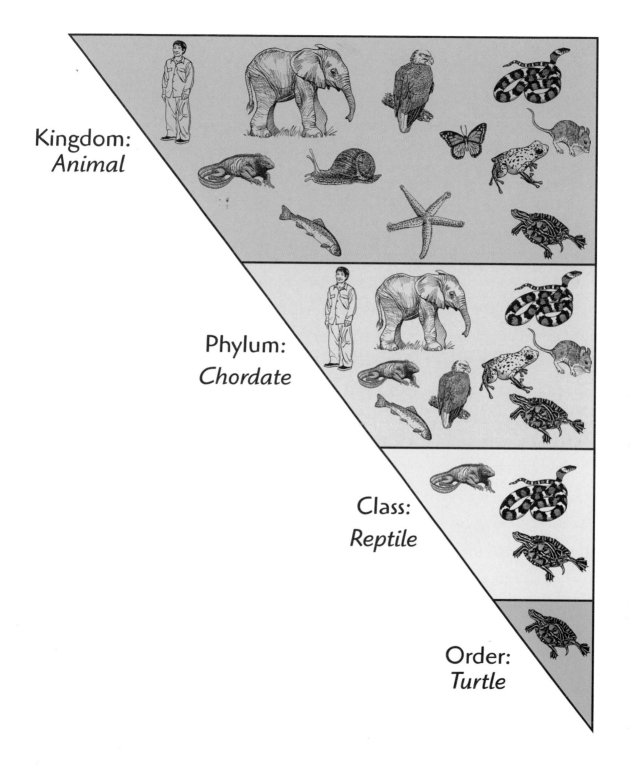

Kingdom:
Animal

Phylum:
Chordate

Class:
Reptile

Order:
Turtle

Musk Turtles

FAMILY: Kinosternidae
COMMON EXAMPLE: Common musk turtle
GENUS AND SPECIES: *Sternotherus odoratus*
SIZE: 3 to 5 3/8 inches (7.5 to 13.5 cm)

If you have ever caught a common musk turtle on your fishing line, you know why some people call it a "stinkpot." When this turtle is upset, it releases a foul-smelling, yellowish liquid. That nasty smell is a great way to drive away its enemies—including you!

Beware! Handling a musk turtle can be dangerous. The males, especially, have bad tempers, and will bite anyone who annoys them. Their long necks can stretch all the way back to their hind legs, so you'll need a pair of heavy gloves to get one off your fishhook.

Even if a pond has a lot of musk turtles, you may never see one. They spend most of their time feeding on small animals or water plants they find on pond bottoms. Even when they sun themselves, these turtles often keep most of their body below the water's surface.

If the water in a pond is very clear, you may be able to see them crawling along the bottom. They look like small stones covered with algae. Look for the yellow stripes on their heads.

If you're lucky, you may spot a stinkpot in a tree. They can climb as high as 6 feet (2 m) along a slanting trunk. If your boat passes underneath the tree, it may spook the sleeping turtle. Imagine having a stinkpot fall on your head!

Snapping Turtles

FAMILY: Chelydridae
COMMON EXAMPLE: Alligator snapping turtle
GENUS AND SPECIES: *Macrocleys temminckii*
SIZE: 15 to 26 inches (38 to 66 cm)

Alligator snapping turtles are the biggest turtles in North America. They may weigh as much as 235 pounds (107 kg)! These turtles get their name from the large bony ridges on their carapace and their swift, savage bite. Never tease or try to pick up a snapping turtle, or you might lose a finger.

An alligator turtle has a special trick for catching fish—a pink, wormlike "lure" on its tongue. The turtle rests on the bottom of the pond with its mouth open and wiggles the lure. When a fish swims up to catch the tasty "worm," the turtle snaps up the victim with its lightning-quick jaws. Besides fish, alligator turtles munch on insects, snails, and frogs. They will even eat other turtles, birds, and small *mammals*.

You might think that big, fierce alligator snappers have no enemies. But they do have one major *predator*—people! During the past 100 years, people have trapped huge numbers of these turtles for food. Recently, however, laws have been passed to protect alligator snappers, so they may yet make a comeback.

Painted Turtles

FAMILY: Emydidae
COMMON EXAMPLE: Eastern painted turtle
GENUS AND SPECIES: *Chrysemys picta*
SIZE: 4 1/2 to 6 inches (11.5 to 15 cm)

Painted turtles are colorful and gentle creatures. That's why some people enjoy keeping them as pets. But painted turtles are much happier living in ponds or slow-moving streams.

Painted turtles love to bask in the sun. Sometimes they gather in large groups and spend the afternoon crowded onto a single log. They need to soak up sunlight to keep their shells strong and healthy. If a painted turtle doesn't get enough sun, its shell becomes soft. Then the turtle will get sick and die.

When they aren't basking in the sun, painted turtles spend most of their time on the muddy bottom of the pond. That's where they find food. They eat plants, insects, crayfish, and snails. They also eat dead animals. Like little sanitation workers, they help keep their pond clean.

In the spring, the male painted turtle courts the female in a way that seems almost human.

16

He stands face to face with his chosen one and strokes her head and neck with his long foreclaws. After the turtles mate, the female lays her eggs on land. The tiny newly hatched turtles are an easy target for hungry birds, so they must scramble, slip, and slide to reach the water as quickly as they can.

Spotted Turtles

FAMILY: Emydidae
COMMON NAME: Spotted turtle
GENUS AND SPECIES: *Clemmys guttata*
SIZE: 3 1/2 to 5 inches (9 to 13 cm)

Like painted turtles, spotted turtles are gentle and brightly colored. If you're in a wetland in the springtime, you may see one sunning itself on a clump of marsh grass. When the turtle spots you, it will slip into the water slowly and quietly. Spotted turtles hardly ever seem to be in a hurry.

In late spring, the females climb up a sunny hillside, dig a shallow, flask-shaped nest in the sandy soil, and lay three to five eggs. In September, the newly hatched turtles scramble out of their nest and scurry to the water. The newborns are only about 1 inch (2.5 cm) long.

Newborn spotted turtles usually have one yellow spot on each scute. But as they grow, they get more and more spots. An old turtle may have more than 100 spots. It's easy to understand why some people call them "polka-dot" turtles.

Sometimes, especially if the weather is cold, the baby turtles decide to stay in the nest all winter. When the spring sun warms the ground, the young turtles pop out and make a mad dash for safety. Although they are an easy target for many predators, plenty of spotted turtles manage to survive and grow to adulthood.

Western Pond Turtles

FAMILY: Emydidae
COMMON EXAMPLE: Pacific pond turtle
GENUS AND SPECIES: *Clemmys marmorata*
SIZE: 3 1/2 to 8 inches (9 to 20 cm)

Pacific pond turtles are the only freshwater turtles that live on the Pacific coast of North America. Their dark-olive, mottled shells make them hard to spot in the muddy waters of the ponds and marshes they like best. Once in a while, you might find one in clear, fast-running mountain streams.

Pacific pond turtles hunt for insects and other small animals during the coolest parts of the day—the evening and early morning. They usually spend the rest of the day lying on the muddy bottom of the pond. They don't bask in the sun as much as painted turtles and spotted turtles, and they almost never share a rock or log with other turtles. If one Pacific pond turtle finds another one hogging its favorite spot, it stretches its neck out, opens its mouth wide,

and flashes its yellow-edged jaws at the intruder. If the turtle is lucky, the trespasser will be scared away.

Pacific pond turtles are hard to catch because they dive for safety at the first sign of danger. Nevertheless, at one time, people trapped and sold them for their tasty meat. By the end of the 1800s, Pacific pond turtles were very rare. Today they are protected by law, so these turtles are becoming more and more common.

Soft-shelled Turtles
FAMILY: Trionychidae
COMMON EXAMPLE: Spiny softshell
GENUS AND SPECIES: *Apalone spiniferus*
SIZE: Males 5 to 9 1/4 inches (13 to 23.5 cm)
Females 6 1/2 to 18 inches (16.5 to 46 cm)

It's easy to recognize a soft-shelled turtle because its round, flat shell is covered with a leathery skin instead of scutes. Its long snout may remind you of a snorkel—and that's just how the soft-shelled turtle uses it. This turtle likes to lie buried in the sand or mud in a shallow part of a pond. When it needs to breathe, it stretches its long neck until its eyes and nose are just above the water's surface.

The soft-shelled turtle is well suited for life in the water. It can absorb oxygen from the water through the blood vessels in its neck. Also, the smooth skin and flexible edges on its shell allow this turtle to swim quite swiftly, and its webbed feet act like paddles to speed it along.

Softshells are great hunters. They have knife-sharp, horny jaws that can catch and hold the most slippery fish. They also eat snails, crabs, crayfish, water insects, worms, and even frogs.

In the spring, the females crawl up on shore to lay their eggs. Each may spend several hours laying as many as thirty eggs in its nest. When the young turtles hatch, they race toward the water and dive to safety.

Snake-necked Turtles
FAMILY: Chelidae
COMMON EXAMPLE: Matamata
GENUS AND SPECIES: *Chelus fimbriatus*
SIZE: 15 1/2 inches (39 cm)

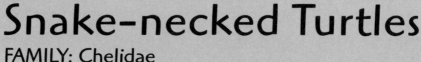

Lurking on the bottom of a shallow, muddy river in South America is the strangest-looking turtle on Earth—the matamata. Its long nose and tiny eyes stick out over its V-shaped mouth. All along its head and neck are fringes of flesh that sway in the current. Its rough carapace is often covered with algae. When the matamata lies still on the river bottom, it looks like a pile of leaves and rubbish.

When its wants to breathe, the matamata stretches its long neck out of the water and takes a breath through its snorkel-like nose. Then it settles down to wait for an unsuspecting fish to swim by. The turtle blends so well with its surroundings that the fish has no idea how much danger it is in. When its unsuspecting prey gets close enough, the matamata stretches out its neck and opens its mouth wide. SWOOSH! The turtle sucks up a big mouthful of water and fish. As soon as the water drains out of the turtle's mouth, it swallows the fish whole.

Young matamatas are more colorful than their parents. They have pink plastrons and pinkish patches on their scutes. As the turtles grow older, their shells darken. Finally, they, too, blend with their muddy surroundings.

Western Swamp Turtles

FAMILY: Chelidae
COMMON NAME: Western swamp turtle
GENUS AND SPECIES: *Pseudemydura umbrina*
SIZE: 5 inches (13 cm)

The little western swamp turtle of Australia is the rarest turtle in the world. Until recently, it had not been seen for more than 100 years, and people thought it was extinct. Then, in 1953, a child found a western swamp turtle outside the city of Perth, Australia. Scientists were very excited and went searching for more. They found about thirty others in two small swamps.

Why are western swamp turtles so rare? As people drained swamps to create new farmland, these turtles lost their winter homes. Their summer homes were destroyed by huge brushfires. And the turtles that managed to find new places to live were often killed by foxes and dogs. Because western swamp turtles lay only three to five eggs a year, they cannot reproduce quickly enough to overcome all these problems.

Can they be saved? Scientists are trying to help. The two swamps where these turtles live have been turned into nature reserves with fox-proof fences. In addition, these turtles are now being *bred* at the Perth Zoo. During the first 6 years of this program, 36 hatchlings survived and were released in the reserves. Scientists will keep on raising turtles in the zoo and then letting them go in the nature reserves. Everyone hopes these efforts will save the western swamp turtle.

Box Turtles

FAMILY: Emydidae
COMMON EXAMPLE: Eastern box turtle
GENUS AND SPECIES: *Terrapene carolina*
SIZE: 4 to 8 1/2 inches (10 to 21.5 cm)

A box turtle has a better suit of armor than any other turtle. A hinge near the middle of its plastron divides it into two movable parts. When the turtle feels threatened, it pulls its head, legs, and tail inside its shell. Then, using powerful muscles, the turtle closes its plastron so tightly that not even a coyote or a raccoon can force the shell open.

Box turtles spend most of their time wandering around grassy woodlands and meadows. When the weather is hot and dry, they often dig a comfortable hole under a rotting log or rest in leaf litter on the forest floor.

Young turtles hatch in the fall, and spend the winter in *hibernation*. By the time spring arrives, the turtles are about 4 inches (10 cm) long—too large to attract raccoons, skunks, or snakes. If a box turtle survives its first spring, it may live to be 40, 60, or even 100 years old.

Box turtles are not picky eaters. They will feed on fruit, berries, tender grasses, slugs, snails, and worms. One of their favorite foods is mushrooms—they can even eat mushrooms that are poisonous to most other animals. In fact, many people have become sick after eating a box turtle that had been dining on poisonous mushrooms. These turtles are tough!

Wood Turtles

FAMILY: Emydidae
COMMON NAME: Wood turtle
GENUS AND SPECIES: *Clemmys insculpta*
SIZE: 5 1/2 to 7 1/2 inches (14 to 19 cm)

If you are wandering in a freshly plowed field, you may come across a wood turtle feasting on the worms that the plow turned up. A look at its carapace will tell you why this turtle is often called the "sculptured" turtle. Each scute is sculptured with ridges that rise to a rough pyramid.

In the summer, wood turtles roam around woods and fields—sometimes far from water—in search of good things to eat. Their favorite food is berries, especially strawberries and blueberries. You can tell when blueberries are in season by the blue stains on a wood turtle's head and feet.

Wood turtles are surprisingly intelligent. People who keep them as pets say that they beg for food like a dog. A hungry wood turtle will approach its owner, stretch out its neck and stand tall on three legs, while holding one of its forelegs in the air until it gets its snack. A scientist who trained wood turtles to run through a maze to reach food found that they performed almost as well as rats.

A wood turtle is more athletic than many other kinds of turtles. If it finds itself on its back, it can quickly flip over and land on its feet. These turtles are also expert climbers—some can even climb a 6-foot (2-m) chain-link fence!

At one time, people hunted these mild-mannered turtles for their meat. By the 1950s, wood turtles had become so rare that many states passed laws to protect them. In the past few decades wood turtles have made a comeback. They are now very common in eastern North America.

Gopher Tortoises

FAMILY: Testudinidae
COMMON NAME: Gopher tortoise
GENUS AND SPECIES: *Gopherus polyphemus*
SIZE: 9 1/4 to 14 1/2 inches (23.5 to 37 cm)

Some people call any land turtle a "tortoise," but only turtles in the testudinidae family are true tortoises. These turtles live on land—often in hot, dry places. Their toes are fused together, and they walk about slowly on stumpy, elephant-like feet.

The gopher tortoise is the only tortoise that lives in North America. Like a gopher, this turtle is an expert *burrow* builder. It digs long slanting underground tunnels that are large enough to turn around in. At the end of each tunnel is a large room where the tortoise rests during the coldest part of the night and the warmest part of the day. The larger a gopher tortoise is, the wider and longer is its burrow. A really big gopher tortoise may dig a tunnel up to 35 feet (11 m) long!

Gopher tortoises come out of their burrows early in the morning to feed on grasses, leaves, fruits, and berries. But when the hot sun begins beating down, they go underground. If these tortoises did not head for shelter, they would overheat and die. When the sun begins to set, the turtles return to the surface to search for more food.

Many animals take advantage of the gopher tortoise's digging skills. Some animals take temporary shelter in tortoise burrows

when it is cold or rainy. Others make these burrows their permanent home. Insects, snakes, frogs, salamanders, lizards, rabbits, opossums, raccoons, and foxes have all been discovered living in burrows dug by a gopher tortoise.

Plow-share Tortoises
FAMILY: Testudinidae
COMMON NAME: Plow-share tortoise
GENUS AND SPECIES: *Geochelone ynipkora*
SIZE: 14 to 17 1/3 inches (35.5 to 44 cm)

The plow-share tortoise gets its name from the shape of its shell, which curves up in the front and looks like the blade of an old-fashioned plow. These turtles live only in eastern Madagascar, but even if you traveled there, you might not see one. The plow-share tortoise is the rarest tortoise in the world—there are only a few dozen left on Earth.

Like the western swamp turtle, this tortoise has lost its habitat as forests have been destroyed to create more farmland. After cutting down the trees, farmers often burn off the smaller trees and bushes, so that nothing is left behind. Also, many tortoises have been killed for food or for their shells.

Although some people are now working to save the plow-share tortoise, it has been very difficult. When scientists in Hawaii tried to breed them, the females laid eggs that never hatched. Eventually, the females laid eggs that did hatch, but the baby turtles grew too quickly and developed deformities.

When scientists in Madagascar tried to breed plow-share tortoises, the females refused to lay eggs. Plow-share tortoises need just the right combination of wet and dry weather in order to reproduce.

Finally, scientists started a breeding program that was more successful. By 1996, 163 baby tortoises had hatched and survived! There may still be hope for the plow-share tortoise.

Terrapins

FAMILY: Emydidae
COMMON EXAMPLE: Diamondback terrapin
GENUS AND SPECIES: *Malaclemys terrapin*
SIZE: Males 4 to 5 1/2 inches (10 to 14 cm)
Females 6 to 9 3/8 inches (15 to 24 cm)

A diamondback terrapin lies on a mud flat in a saltwater marsh. It is basking in the hot, midday sun. The sun does more than just warm the turtle. It also heats up the pesky barnacles that have attached themselves to the turtle's shell. Eventually, the barnacles die.

Diamondbacks are never found far from saltwater bays and marshes. They cruise the waterways in search of crabs, marine worms, shellfish, and dead fish. By rapidly kicking their webbed back feet, diamondbacks can swim along at quite a pace.

A diamondback's jaws are amazingly strong. They can easily crunch through the shells of horse mussels and other shellfish. They can even shatter the hard shells of periwinkles.

In May and June, females lay their eggs in a remote spot. The hatchlings are so frail and tiny—about the size of a quarter—that it's hard to imagine how they survive. They are easy prey for long-legged herons and sharp-eyed eagles as well as hungry fish and alligators. You may never see a diamondback hatchling in the wild, no matter how hard you look. They know how to hide from all their predators!

About 100 years ago, people captured and killed diamondbacks

for their tasty meat. Because female diamondbacks are not ready to lay eggs until they are 7 years old, many turtles were caught before they even had young. Today, these turtles are protected by law, and they have begun to make a comeback.

Leatherback Turtles

FAMILY: Dermochelidae
COMMON NAME: Leatherback turtle
GENUS AND SPECIES: *Dermochelys coriacea*
SIZE: 50 to 84 inches (127 to 213 cm)

Among sea turtles, the leatherback turtles hold all the records. They grow bigger, travel farther, and swim in colder waters than any of their relatives. The largest leatherback turtle ever measured was 10 feet (3 m) long. Each year, these turtles swim thousands of miles from the tropics—where they nest—to the chilly waters off Newfoundland.

A leatherback looks different from other turtles, too. Its shell is covered with leathery skin instead of horny scutes. It looks as though a piece of black rubber has been tightly stretched over the turtle's body. The shell underneath is made of a thin layer of bone, rather than bony plates. The leatherback is the only turtle with a backbone that is not connected to its shell.

Leatherbacks are well suited to life in deep ocean waters. Their long, smooth, flexible bodies are perfectly streamlined. They are protected from the icy northern waters by a thick layer of oily fat.

Their favorite food is jellyfish, which is not easy to catch or eat. It's like trying to hunt living Jell-O. But leatherbacks have razor-sharp jaws with deep notches—perfect for holding and slicing their slippery, quivering prey. They even have spiny structures inside their throats to keep the jellyfish from sliding back out.

At nesting time, females must heave their huge, heavy bodies up onto land. As they move along the sandy beach, pebbles scrape their tender skin and make them bleed. Imagine how relieved these turtles must be when they have laid their eggs and can return to their ocean home.

Ridleys
FAMILY: Cheloniidae
EXAMPLE: Kemp's ridley
GENUS AND SPECIES: *Lepidochelys kempii*
SIZE: 23 1/2 to 29 1/2 inches (60 to 75 cm)

With its neck outstretched and its jaws open wide, a ridley chases a blue crab along the ocean floor. The turtle flaps its flipperlike legs madly. Like the rudder on a boat, the turtle's rear flippers help it turn to follow its scuttling *prey*. The crab waves its large claws to scare off its attacker. But these claws are no match for the tough-skinned ridley's powerful jaws. Suddenly, the ridley lunges forward, grabs the crab, and crunches through its shell.

Ridleys also like to eat shrimp. Unfortunately for the turtle, where there are shrimp, there are also shrimpers— with nets. As the huge funnel-shaped nets sweep the ocean floor, they trap everything in their path—incluiding rid-leys. The turtles struggle desperately to break free from the nets, but they soon run out of breath and drown.

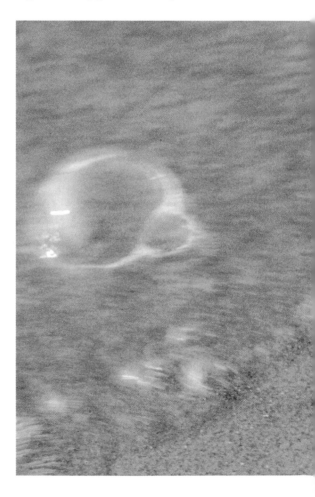

Shrimpers are not the only danger that ridleys face. All ridleys build their nests and lay eggs on the same remote beach in Mexico. Unfortunately, people living on the island often steal the turtle eggs and sell them. In some cases, these people have even slaughtered the female turtles and sold their skins, which are used to make leather handbags and gloves. Although these turtles and their nesting sites are now protected, the number of ridleys continues to drop. Is it too late for them to recover?

Saving the Turtles

For millions of years, turtles have thrived all over the world. Although the hatchlings often fell prey to hungry predators, adult turtles were protected by their tough shells.

During the last 100 years, however, turtles have faced a new predator—humans. Some people gathered turtle eggs to eat or to sell.

Others killed adult turtles to meet the huge demand for their meat and for green turtle soup. Handbags, belts, and shoes were made from their leathery skins, and cooking oils and cosmetics were made from their oil. People also wanted their shells to make jewelry. As the turtle industry grew, and as the natural habitats of many turtles were destroyed, the turtle population began to shrink.

Humans also caused other problems for turtles. Sea turtles were often caught in shrimpers' nets. Turtles that hunt jellyfish often swallowed floating pieces of plastic that clogged their intestines and killed them.

It took a long time, but eventually, people began to realize the effect they were having on turtle populations. They passed laws that protect turtles and preserve their habitats. In 1973, it became illegal in the United States to kill sea turtles or take their eggs. Some other countries also try to protect them. But even after these laws were enacted, the turtle population continued to drop.

As more and more people became worried about sea turtles, new laws were passed. Shrimpers were forced to attach "turtle excluder devices" to their nets. Ships can no longer throw their garbage overboard, so there is less plastic debris to tempt the turtles.

People set up programs to monitor and protect turtle nests. Volunteers patrol the beaches at night. When a female turtle has laid her eggs, the volunteers dig up the eggs and take them to safe hatcheries on dark beaches that are surrounded by electric fences. When the hatchlings start their scramble for the sea, the volunteers are there to protect them from enemies. And when the young turtles are ready to lay eggs of their own, they return to the safe beach where they hatched.

Of course, many turtles living on land are in trouble, too. Scientists have recently started to help western swamp turtles, plowshare tortoises, and others. Thanks to the people who care about these ancient creatures and are working hard to save them, there is now new hope for the turtles of the world.

Words to Know

burrow—a shelter dug in the ground.

bred—chose specific animals to mate and have young in order to create an animal with a particular appearance or behavior.

carapace—the upper part of a turtle's shell.

class—a group of creatures within a phylum that share certain characteristics.

cold-blooded—having a body temperature that changes with the temperature of the animal's surroundings.

family—a group of creatures within an order that share certain characteristics.

genus (plural **genera**)—a group of creatures within a phylum that share certain characteristics.

habitat—the environment where a plant or animal lives and grows.

hibernation—spending the winter in a deep sleep, with slowed heart rate and breathing.

kingdom—one of the five divisions into which all living things are placed: the animal kingdom, the plant kingdom, the fungus kingdom, the moneran kingdom, and the protist kingdom.

mammal—an animal that has a backbone and feeds its young with mother's milk.

order—a group of creatures within a class that share certain characteristics.

phylum (plural **phyla**)—a group of creatures within a kingdom that share certain characteristics.

plastron—the lower part of a turtle's shell.

predator—an animal that catches and feeds on other animals.

prey—an animal hunted for food by another animal (a predator).

reptile—an animal that lives on land, lays eggs, and is cold-blooded. Examples include alligators, turtles, snakes, and lizards.

scute—a horny plate on a turtle's shell.

species—a group of creatures within a genus that share certain characteristics. Members of the same species can mate and produce young.

warm-blooded—having a body temperature that is internally regulated. Humans are warm-blooded and maintain a body temperature close to 98.6°F (37°C).

Learning More

Books

Arnold, Caroline. *Sea Turtles*. New York: Scholastic, 1994.

Baskin-Salzberg, Anita, and Allan Salzberg. *Turtles*. New York: Franklin Watts, 1996.

Berger, Melvin. *Look Out for Turtles*. New York: HarperCollins, 1992.

Conant Roger, Joe Collins, and Robert C. Stebbens. *Peterson First Guide to Reptiles and Amphibians*. Boston: Houghton Mifflin, 1992.

Donnati, Annabelle. *Golden Guide to Reptiles and Amphibians*. Racine, WI: Western Publishing, 1993.

White, William. *All About the Turtle*. New York: Sterling Publishing, 1992.

Web Sites

This page, which is part of the University of Michigan Museum of Zoology's web site, lists a variety of turtles. To learn more about any one of these species, just click on the highlighted text.
http://www.oit.itd.umich.edu/bio108/Chordata/Reptilia/Testudines.shtml

This site includes turtle trivia, specific information about some turtles, as well as links to sites that describe conservation efforts, how to build a turtle pond, and more.
http://www.xmission.com/~gastown/herpmed/chelonia.htm

Index

About the Author

Sara Swan Miller has enjoyed working with children all her life, first as a Montessori nursery school teacher, and later as an outdoor environmental educator at the Mohonk Preserve in New Paltz, New York. As the director of the Preserve school program, she has led hundreds of children on field trips and taught them the importance of appreciating and respecting the natural world.

She has written a number of children's books including *Three Stories You Can Read to Your Dog*; *Three Stories You Can Read to Your Cat*; *What's in the Woods?: An Outdoor Activity Book*; *Oh, Cats of Camp Rabbitbone*; *Piggy in the Parlor and Other Tales*; *Better Than TV*; and *Will You Sting Me? Will You Bite?: The Truth About Some Scary-Looking Insects*. She has also written several other books in the Animals in Order series.